Cactus as Bad Boy

Cactus as Bad Boy

Poems by

Susan Vespoli

Cover by Shay Culligan
Cover art by Vladimir Melnik
Author photo by John Dooley

ISBN: 978-1-63980-096-4

Kelsay Books
502 South 1040 East, A-119
American Fork, Utah 84003
Kelsaybooks.com

This book is dedicated to my teachers:
Tina Barry, Richard Garcia, Laurie Wagner,
and Pema Chodron; to the Wild Writing
community, to the C.O.W.s,
to my granddaughter Molly,
and to John.

bad boy | [bad boi] | *adj & noun, slang*

1 Rebel, one who isn't afraid to break the rules.
2 Confident, brave, dominant, and assertive male.
3 Flirty, knows what to say to women and that's his superpower.
4 Man commonly seen atop a motorcycle.
5 Sexually desirable but offers high chance of heartbreak.
6 Can also refer to a car or excellent specimen of something.

Acknowledgments

Grateful acknowledgment is made to the following journals, where versions of these pieces have appeared or are forthcoming.

"After Flying in a Yellow Plane to the San Diego Airport"
  —*dancing girl press*
"Another Nice Thing About Dogs"
  —*Monsoon Voices, A Quiet Shelter There*
"At the Granite Creek Vineyards in Chino"
  —*dancing girl press*
"Bagged During Quarantine"
  —*Boston Literary Mag*
"Dating Again—Double-Abecedarian-2007"
  —*dancing girl press*
"Even Bodhisattvas Get the Blues"
  —*dancing girl press*
"Ferry Ride"
  —*The Poet Mag*
"Haiku in Solitude"
  —*Writers.com Spring Community Journal*
"He Lusts After Librarians"
  —*OVS Magazine*
"I'm the Screamer in the Munch Painting"
  —*Muddy River Review*
"Long Term Relationship"
  —*dancing girl press*
"Motorcycle Road Trip Through Six States"
  —*New Verse News*
"On the One-Year Anniversary of Your Exit"
  —*The Poet Mag*
"Remember Triolet"
  —*dancing girl*

"Sea Otters"
    —*Kind of a Hurricane Press*
"Thinking About Love During COVID & Coups"
    —*New Verse News*
"USA in ABCs"
    —*South85 Journal*
"Wanted"
    —*Grand Little Things*

Contents

IV.

I.

Cactus as Bad Boy

"And yet, despite all the warnings and red flags, the pull of dating a bad boy was just too strong."

—Dina Cheney, author

Cacti. Opuntia. Prickly Pear. Hair-fine thorns
cover my limbs, yet she leans toward my lavender
paddles, buds on orbs ripe to burst.
Edible fruit. Arms open to sun, heat
leads to blind spots. Wise mind shrinks
like the pollen-drunk bees that revel
in petal cups, on feathery stamen, sepal.

Drones rub abdomens, dive, somersault. Poise stinger.
Watch her press palm to plant, despite cacta-flesh
needle-thin spines. Finger a yellow flower
so bright it glows before it wilts.

Cycle of the blossom.   One day.   Come on.
Lodged in skin, I stay.   *Spike. Glochid. Prick.*

Dating Again Double-Abecedarian—2007

All freed up minding my own biz.
Been contained for thirty
cantankerous ones in the marital box.
Delighted to be single? And how!
Eating veggie sans harassment, no T.V.
fracturing my peace. But then I met you.
"Go to Dharmamatch.com." instructed my therapist.
"Hone your be-nice-to-men skills."
In doubt, ME: cynical dating amateur:
joined. Perused all candidates for humor and I.Q.
Kind of liked your profile and mastery of the sarcastic quip.
Lengthy, laughing emails made us pen pals. We were simpatico!
Man, it was perfect. Relationship Lite. You, three months out of
    town.
No worries, pressures...and then WHAM!
Out of the blue, you check into a local hotel.
"Perhaps we could meet today," you write, "...to talk."
Quietly, I drown my gut's butterflies in morning O.J.
Really, why not? A note for the F.B.I.
should help solve my missing person's case. Ugh!
That would be sobering.
Utilizing my stash of calm, I say "sure." Internally, I scoff
violently at your suggestion of meeting for coffee,
wanting an ample cannon of tequila and
Xanax, instead. Externally, I mimic
your nonchalance as we gab,
zeroing in on location of our first date: Pepe's Taco Villa.

At the Granite Creek Vineyards in Chino

the peacock
leans his head back
to laugh like a raucous cat.

A showgirl in cobalt,
he wears a headdress
made from brilliant Q-tips

struts on twig legs
in white tights
across the sunlit lawn

to nibble crackers
from my outstretched hand
with the same surprising gentleness
you use to hold mine.

Let Us Vaccinate Ourselves

against cherophobia, the fear of joy,
by adopting a 3-legged Shih Tzu
from the pound. Let him be

our role model: 15 pounds
of dirt-coated curly fur
on a wad of gum.

Let us take him to Dog Beach
over Spring Break
so we can watch him hurtle

up and down the expanse of light
tan sand while laughing
through his crooked underbite,

as he attempts to hump German Shepherds,
steal balls from labs, and chases
a white poodle in a pink dress

all the way to the parking lot,
while the little thing's owner runs
after her, calling, *Fifi, Fifi!*

while cursing our pup
who finally stops at the curb,
panting, smiling at us

like we're his best friends
as we lean over to snap on
his red retractable leash.

USA in ABCs

Armadillos belly up on tar as we buzz
by hoping for roadkill's reincarnation along freeway.
Cars have turned wildlife eyes into double x
dead ones that we see through our lack of car window.
Eyeful of everything from a blue motorcycle. We rev
five days through six states, thank you
gods of traveling erect
hunching around lover's back, belt loops
inserted with thumb and forefinger,
jeans stronger than seat belts. Trusting maps, I.Q.,
karma and experience, surrounding him with my lap,
leaning on his silent form, branched arms and torso,
my chest, our bodies press across the nation
nodding to southern states' beauty and blight, vroom
of Kawasaki, encased in helmet, black vinyl shell,
perched. Legs circling leather, cargo strapped to back.
Quartet of convicts on cleanup, realtors named B.J.,
radioactive hot springs, tractor-mowed grass waving its smell. I
see persistently grazing cows, badgers
    and towns that have met death,
tornado-ed streets spread out like a rug
under disaster clipped trees, a scalped roof
very intact, lying in the front lawn of its house.
Wide panoramas, flat and steep, canyons
    and cornfields slashed by road,
x-icons brought back by statuary, museums, diner
    shrines without AC.
Yesterday's musicians play on: Elvis, Tina Turner,
Loretta Lynn, and B.B.
Zipping past Graceland, Pie Town, Hateful Hussey's Café
    on the way home to Arizona.

Motorcycle Road Trip Through Six States

Riding in the wake of his confidence
sheltered by shoulders and back
contained in a capsule of body slapping
wind, rain pellets and unexpected air.

Sheltered by shoulders and back
roads, tires grab streets that
wind. Rain pellets and unexpected air
bombs nose with aftershave, barbecue, trails of pot.

Roads, tires grab streets that
cut mountains, towns on map gone ghost,
bombed. No more aftershave, barbecue. Trails of pot
holes, weeds, and dark windows boarded up.

Cut mountains, towns on map gone ghost,
waitresses and desk clerks without teeth smile through
holes, weeds and dark windows boarded up.
Shrubbery and crabgrass push through asphalt.

Waitresses and desk clerks without teeth, smile through
poverty; paint praying Jesus murals on hotel stucco,
Shrubbery and crabgrass push through asphalt,
optimistic signs, still readable and hanging.

Poverty paints praying Jesus. Murals on hotel stucco,
customers, hotel guests, gas pumps pried up.
Optimistic signs still readable and hanging
"We're here for you" and "winner."

Customers, gas pumps, hotel guests pried up,
washed away by economic tide, presidents
"We're here for you" and "winner."
Red against blue, black against white, political snits leave victims.

Motorcycle slices view of a country
contained in a capsule of body slapping
holding on to what works: lovers, politicos or Jesus.
Riding in the wake of his confidence

Opening

The back of the world
has caught light
and will soon peel back
its morning rind of bed jacket
to offer up its segments
to be pulled apart.

II.

Another Nice Thing about Dogs

is their lack
of an index finger
to point out
our multiple inadequacies
or to aim
at a list of shoulds.

No trigger finger
to set us off.
No questions.
No answers.
Just the eternal mink stole
of their acceptance.

The only long, slender digit
that they wag
is their tail
which sluices
through our moods
like a windshield wiper
in a storm.

I'm the Screamer in the Munch Painting

Turns out I have a temper.
Yes, it's a shock to me, too.
Look at my OMG facial expression,
mouth in the *Oh!* position. Palms
to my cheeks in the *My-God,*
I thought I was perfect. Oh, sure,
I'm a fan of colorful language,
a freak for the F word,
(Don't ask me to give up the F word.)
But, imperfect?

Can I forgive me?
Even heaven throws tantrums.
Watch her lob flame spears of blood
and orange. And the ocean? How she
froths while throttling the pier. So, yes.
I'm a screamer when angry,
and though I don't have devil horns
or a pitchfork, I've learned my wings
are just scapula. And, a halo? Never
had one, just this human dome of flesh
over skull that flashes with furious light.

Argues

Calm is my mantra, my anti-ager.
Anger makes cortisol levels surge,

turns teetotaler into booze user,
salad eater into cookie snarfer,

not sage ways to douse rage.
No. I will take the saner

route. Don my piss gear
against the storm. Avoid ague

with Om as my ruse,
breathe in and out sugar

to sweeten bitterness
in we who argue.

Sugar Song

"Is sugar a substitute for love?" ~ a 12-step sponsor

Lift the lid from gold
box of See's chocolates
dusted with coconut,
flecked with jimmies,
sprinkles. Who can resist bite-
size bliss in crinkled paper skirts?

Pop gingerbread-barn
from plastic and cardboard
for grandgirl to assemble:
cookie walls, roof, silo, two bags
of icing to knead till spreadable,
a candy cow, pig, sheep,
and tiny tube of decorative black gel.

Watch her frost farm walls red,
shingle rooftop with gum drops,
marzipan berries, outline windows
from the snipped tip of the pinched tube,
                then slip under the table,
where she sucks it like a teat, grins up
from the floor, her lips and teeth dyed black.

Dear Our Lady of Slow Learners

O, divine advice giver, please reply
with breadcrumbs of insight

to octane my unicursal snail crawl
through the labyrinth of fogginess

where I trek for wisdom,
yet bump into the same dead end.

If you could send a new optical prescription
or list of tips, I will fold and carry

them in the zippered side pouch
of my purse like a talisman.

Your face tilts in my mind's eye,
lids at half-mast over sad brown irises,

brows raised in a *tsk, tsk,*
lips, though puckered,   tight,   form a tiny pink heart,

      which kind of gives me hope.

Googling the Crane Fly

And now I know what they are:
giant bite-less mosquito
look-alikes circling the campfire
of our bathroom nightlight.

Giant bite-less mosquitoes
are called crane flies, drawn to water
and our bathroom's nightlight.
They look like strands of hair in flight,

bird cranes flocking to water—
mystical symbols of good fortune.
But oh! My hair strands take flight
when bugs join me in the shower.

Mystical symbols of good fortune,
Wikipedia says your mission is to mate
in the singles bar of my shower.
Well, go for it. I won't squish you.

If your mission is to mate, killing
those looking for love seems bad karma,
because aren't we all? I won't squish you.
Now I know who you are.

Even Bodhisattvas Get the Blues

Pema Chodron, a Buddhist nun
who teaches peace and compassion worldwide,

once threw a rock at the forehead
of her former husband—

which gives me hope.

Even though I meditate,
listen to self-help CDs,

mediate conflicts at work,
where a large BE HAPPY sign
hangs over my desk,

at home I roll my eyes,
slam doors, and pepper
my sentences with expletives.

And when you, oh love of my life,
say that after all your training as a therapist,

you *certainly* know how to communicate
with me, who reminds you of a wet cat,

I can't help but snap:
Well, your skills still suck with me,

the middle finger of my voice
rising like a whack-a-mole.

Ordering a Cheese Enchilada at Otro Cafe
on 7th Street

Our waitress jiggles
around our table
like a bowl of ripe fruit,
brings salsa, chips,
leans over, makes eye
contact with my date,
giggles, *of course, I can
memorize your order* and I am
hungry for cheese enchiladas
and my date is all rooster
at her shimmy and bounce,
all googly-eyed at her
cantaloupes in a bra
and I say, *I'll have a cheese
enchilada with green sauce*
and she is all floor show
at the Kitty Kat Lounge
on Grand Avenue
and he is all patron with a fat
wallet of ones and I am hungry
for a cheese enchilada.
When she finally twirls
plates back to our table,
mine holds chunks
of broccoli, spears
of zucchini that poke
out of the tortilla
like a middle finger
and I say, *what is that?*

My date rolls his eyes
at the buzzkill of my question,
and the waitress blinks, seeing me
for perhaps the first time, asks,
you didn't order a veggie enchilada?

Day Lilies

on our table
have about reached their end.
So fresh with potential
when you brought them home
from Safeway some weeks ago.

An astounding blossom or two
would emerge daily
from snug green sleeping bags,
yellow petals fluttering
above split cocoons.

And now, each flower
disassembles itself
before dropping limp parts
to our kitchen table.

We are as happy as dead flowers,
pleased to have flown at all.

III.

Your Right Foot

I dreamed I shot off all your toes,
one bullet for each lipstick tube
and in each spot grew a perfect rose.
I pulled the trigger, blossoms opened:
pink buds popped; red petals bloomed.
I dreamed I shot off all your toes,
one bullet for each lipstick tube.

Ferry Ride

Crazy about ripples and light bouncing off
the surface of Puget Sound. Crazy about John

who spots seals bobbing like humans in swim caps,
points to a silvery curved back

and tail that swoops above the water line,
says: "A whale!" as the ferry captain booms

over a loudspeaker, "Orcas at the bow!"
and the passengers rise from their perches

to swarm the deck as the orca tucks itself
under water. And the throng in wool caps,

hoodies, and raincoats wave their phones in the air,
shouting, "Where? Where? Where?"

Roundabout Roads: UK

The road is a cleavage in bosoms of green
and the signage playfully taunts us.
Roundabout, roundabout, roundabout. Sheep!

"Go left." No. "Go right." No. "Go straight!" signs scream.
Narrowly leading past angry red bus,
the road is a cleavage in bosoms of green.

Pygmy goats grazing by flocks of wild geese,
cattle are swallowing hillsides of grass.
Roundabout, roundabout, roundabout. Sheep!

Castles, cathedrals, and abbeys, the Queen
smiles from her souvenir teacups and mugs.
The road is a cleavage in bosoms of green.

Right-sided steering wheel, left side of street,
scolding voice snaps at us, Brit GPS.
Roundabout, roundabout, roundabout. Sheep!

Hold on tight, buckle up, enjoy the scene—
flowering countryside sliced through by us.
The road is a cleavage in bosoms of green.
Roundabout, roundabout, roundabout. Sheep!

He Lusts after Librarians

their long, dull hair contained
by clips and bands of elastic
so ready to uncoil into shimmer;

deep pools of azure
peering over spectacles
of wired rim, tortoise shell or plastic;

a vast ocean of info
swims beneath jackets,
between covers,
bookended by hard backs and soft.

They know everything
or at least where to find it—
secrets of mankind
waiting in tomes
to be explored
by the deft flick of their hands.

Each lifts a single finger
to pouting painted lips
drawn into a small tight circle
of shush.

They appear stern, closed,
but he reads them differently:
as simply being overdue
with need
to be pulled from shelf,
held with human hands
and opened.

Electricity Is the Presence and Flow
of Electric Charge

2007

Blue jeans, blue eyes, black shirt, straight teeth: you smile
at me in Pepe's booth. I grin at you.
You hold your hand out, take a breath, say, "Susan?"
I nod and touch your palm, then blush (I'm shy)
as currents, ohms, and voltage from you fly
into my fingers. Fire! Sparks! I swoon
as mariachis circle us with tune.
We order margaritas, chips. You buy.

2019

Flash forward twelve years: you walk through the door
like clockwork, toss your shoes, drape clothes on chair,
ask, "How's your day?" with offhand glance at me
who sits on sofa watching you cross floor
to put your arms around me, touch my cheek,
then ZAP I feel it: electricity.

Travel

I want to travel back to a time when we traveled.
I want to sit on that cliff above Devil's Churn
and watch water thrash like the inside of a blender

on pulverize. I want to lie back on the pointy meringue
peaks of triangular pillows tilted by the German maid
who unlocked our hotel door with a brass key.

I want to dip my oar into the Colorado River
and watch the bridge by Hoover Dam shrink
into toothpicks behind our canoe. I want to pedal

that bicycle-built-for-two along the river walk
in Little Rock, meet you in Nashville and climb aboard
your motorcycle to race hurricanes home. I want the Atlantic

to splash and wave at us up on the balcony of a high-rise
in Nags Head during off-season. But instead, I wake alone
at 3 a.m., two small dogs and a once-a-week granddaughter
as my travel-mates, no map, armed with intuition, internet,
    intention

to rise to the occasion, you in a house 15-hundred miles
away, waiting for a vaccine to feel safe around me,
sending me an email of a YouTube: The Temptations
"I Can't Get Next to You."

Holy Penis

"Bhutan's phallic worship is getting a second look."
—Tara Limbu, The Washington Post

Artists carve wood
and bone into erect
penises in Bhutan,
paint them bright hues,
give them teeth, eyes,
call them holy, mural
walls and temples with
what one lama called
his flaming thunderbolt.
I've gone in and out
of love with the penis,
depending on who it
was attached to. Once
I modeled a replica of
a lover's phallus from
clay, glue, yarn, and a
wooden plaque I bought
at a craft store, kneaded
the medium into a totem,
measured it for size
with my mouth, mounted
it between two smooth stones
from my yard, and when it
hardened, painted it the perfect
hue, then kept that statue in my
bedroom until I lost faith, broke
up with the man and tossed my
shrine to his shlong into a Rubber-
maid can at the curb, watching
with regret as a trash truck swallowed
the relic and rumbled away.

Thinking about Love During COVID & Coups

I've been thinking about the Hopi Prophecy as told to me
by a friend, how we would find ourselves in a rushing river,
our body a soggy vessel careening toward the unknown; the Hopi
instruction was to notice who traveled beside us, not to flail

or cling to the shore, but to trust the water. I've been thinking
about the deep bass voice & compelling smell of an armpit, a man
who sang lyrics into my ear, leaned around me as I washed a pan,
crooned, *I just can't live without you, sister golden hair surprise,*

how he vanished with that torso he'd spooned around me,
strapped into his own life vest, his SUV growing smaller
as it exited the street in front of my house where I've stayed
mostly alone since March, and how the ones who've held

my hand and head above water have done so through Zoom
screens or contained in chiweenie fur or while flouncing around
the living room in a size 6x little girl's net skirt. How comfort
has come via iPhones on speaker, text boxes, Words with Friends

app chats, or from the masked employees at Jiffy Lube,
a uniformed ballet of them who unscrew, drain, pour fluid,
bow, you're welcome, smile with eyes, say, you're okay now,
reset the Need Maintenance light that flashed on my dash.

Ring Finger

The tip of my thumb
still reaches across

my palm's life line, heart
line, head line, stretches

over the Girdle of Venus
to touch the tender

base of Apollo, circling it,
surprised by the absence

of the glittery band, although
it's been gone for months.

Circumference of skin
still stunned to be naked

of the symbol, bauble, ballast,
zirconium disco ball,

although a rash rippled
the derma when I wore it,

pink bumps that prickled
into what I now see

were red flags.

Tangled

Cords behind the flat screen
that end up plugged into the wrong
holes.   Poodle fur curly cues
clung to by sticker-burrs the size
of metal snaps.   Phone calls
with loved ones where I tiptoe
around the topic of my adult
kids, niceties draped over elephant
in the room.   Granddaughter's long
mocha hair, smooth on top, snarled
underneath into knots I try to pick
apart with a brush. Intimate coupling
with the lover of almost 15 years
who tells me he doesn't divulge
to others he is in a relationship,
calls himself a feral cat.

Sea Otters

Sea otters hold hands while they're sleeping
so they don't drift away from each other;

lying on their backs, they float through night
like kayaks rafted together by tow ropes,

lulled by the cradling rock of waves that roll
from flat to round to pointy peaks of foam.

And I think that's what I miss the most.
Lying on my back with you dozing beside me,

your hand draped over my heart like a gentle tent,
my fingers laced through yours in a sort of truce,

because when we slept no one had to be right.

Long Term Relationship

Although we've been together
for ten years minus two breakups
and are now what he used to mock
with an eye roll and call an LTR,
I still get goosebumps
when he hugs me,
and when I set the table
with plates of salmon
and chard from the garden,
he lights the candle,
we sit down and look
across at each other,

and our two neutered dogs
start rolling around the floor
like Frida and Diego,
biting each other's necks,
licking muzzles, locking teeth,
taking turns lying on their backs
exposing bellies, bowing shoulders
while lifting backsides and moaning
a wild guttural animal song
until it reaches a crescendo,
and they curl up together
in one of their two dog beds
encircled in each other's
paws and go to sleep.

Wanted

My therapist says, *love addiction,* but is that true
if I only jones for one specific guy?
Don't contact, I've been told. *He's wrong for you,*
by friends and family, Bob the psychic, and I comply.

His kids don't like me either, watched their dad hurt.
My shrink plugs online dating as a cure: *Try to open.*
See who's out there. But years ago, I tried, and found worse:
men who lied, stunk of mothballs, begged for S&M.

I wonder if my ex was that bad or my interpretation?
When I make a list of what I want today, he gets a 90%.
I type my specs for perfection into a Google search, then wait
for a mix of David Byrne, Colbert, and Leonard Cohen,

but, up pops a photo of a robot and a woman, holding hands.
In my spam, my ex's email: *I still love you, oh, dear Susan.*

Remember Triolet

Remember how we joined our lips
welted skin by melding mouths?
Tasting sweet and salty spit,
remember how we joined our lips?
I felt you through my denim hips
roses budding under blouse.
Remember how we joined our lips
welted skin by melding mouths?

IV.

Bagged During Quarantine

"You didn't bother to tell me before I drove two-and-a-half hours to visit?"
—Me

How'd he quit the relationship?
By removing gold ring from his left finger.
Susie-Sunshine-Can-Be-Stupid
asks, "Where's your ring?"
"Stopped wearing it," his reply
while taking another bite of salad.
"Too little time together." Utterly
nonchalant with an especially passive
undertone of violence. Or was that me
who wanted to smash that glass
Buddha head into my now X's noggin,
a man still forking fish from plate
to mouth, a man who X-ed me out
without even mentioning it?

All his clothes and shoes bagged
in Hefty black plastic. Closet emptied
and wiped down of his smell, like after
a death, except he's still breathing
up in Flagstaff. Fucker used to be
a good word, not a slur. "Pour
your hormone replacement
purple ovals into the trash
and you won't miss him," jokes
my friend, like it's estrogen,
not his kiss, voice, fingertips
that tripped the lust switch.

Fangs

Molly holds two orange-striped bugs in the air
linked like jewelry, says, "Look! They're eating each other."
Probably having good bug sex, I think, but say, "Be careful."

More captives to join the leaf-winged moth
now living in a pickle jar on a frisbee that she sails
around her pink plastic pool as we watch the sky turn orange,

then darken. By our second night, she hears my, "Time for a bath,"
"Pick three books to read," and "Brush your teeth," like Charlie
Brown hears all adults: the *wahwahwah* of a trombone
with a mute in its bell.

When the lights are finally out, I sigh, think, *I need some
pampering, a massage, some chocolate cake,* as she grabs her
flashlight to search for spiders in the hall.
When her finger and thumb hover

over a Daddy Long Legs, even I'm surprised when my
slippered toe squishes her target. "Grandma!" she shrieks,
and I shrug, google my defense, read it to her, "See, they're
poisonous," yet don't read, "but their fangs are too short
to hurt humans." Unlike mine.

Mitt Romney Chin

John asking even before the pandemic
if I was going to watch my granddaughter
EVERY Wednesday / John buying a house
in Flagstaff, so we can go back and forth
depending on the season / John saying in March,
"You're putting my life in danger," when I say I
don't want to be one more loss in her life / John hiking
forests with the widow of his friend, unworried
about her contagion / John going on daily walks
with his new neighbor, a divorced nurse / John asking me
to bring up his good pots and pans / John saying he wants us
to divide the furnishings to "make each of us whole" / John
insisting, "No, I'm not breaking up with you, you're most
welcome here" /John insisting, "It's all in your head" / John
wearing a mask, lying naked on what used to be our bed /
John removing a doorknob to see if the opening could be a glory
hole / John asking how soon I can drive back up / John calling
his healthcare provider, a woman who isn't really his doctor
anymore, asking her if he can catch COVID from my spit
on his skin / John taking a call on his porch from someone
named Linda /John saying he didn't like the crust on the pie
I'd baked, so fed it to the dog / John whispering, *no one will
ever love you like I do* / John not asking about my daughter
who was just scooped up by police and committed to a psych
ward /John following me to my car after I've loaded five or six
armfuls of my belongings / John telling me I have too much drama
in my life / John saying it's all in my head / John's jaw drop
when I say, "That's called gaslighting; stop it" / John holding
out his hand for his key / John clicking on his flashlight to search
after I throw it / John saying, "Stop making so much noise,
my neighbors will hear you, and I'm respected around here."

Breakup as End of the World

I remember being seven, watching a man
carry a sign that read "The World Is Ending"
and I wondered, *is that true?* Here I am

still wondering.   What I do know
is the Dollar Store sells mega-packs of bubbles
I buy for my five-year-old granddaughter

to blow in the bathtub, and the plastic wands
are all different. Some have tiny holes,
some big figure-eights, and others

chains of ovals and she has mastered her breath
to propel multiple-mini-bubbles into the air
above the water or she can conjure conical

ovoids that morph into Os, but the most impressive
come when I pour shampoo into her hand
and she puts her palms together, and exhales

to create grand-finale, rubber-ball-size
orbs that float before they pop, and when she rubs
the remaining puddle of soap into her hair
                                        she laughs.

On the One-Year Anniversary of Your Exit

Because I didn't want to miss you, I cut
my hair and saged the house. Because I didn't want
to miss you, I dragged the futon mattress you slept on

that last night to the curb. Because I didn't want
to miss you, I heaped every flavor of Tillamook
onto a nightly cone, sometimes two, then I licked

them. Because I didn't want to miss you, I rode my bike
hundreds of laps around neighborhood blocks. Note: I
still ring that little round silver bell on the handlebars

you brought back from Japan. Because I didn't want to miss
you, I emptied my cupboards of all the dishes we'd dined on
and bought new ones, plus trashed the candles you'd lit.

Because I didn't want to miss you, I tore off our bed sheets
and bought a pink set. Because I didn't want to miss you,
I Goodwilled clothes you liked and kept the ones you didn't;

"You're still wearing THAT?" you said as you rolled
your eyes. Because I didn't want to miss you, I chanted OM
to blank out your face. Because I didn't want to miss you,

I put photos of us in a bottom drawer, face down,
where I also shoved that post-it note you wrote and tacked
on my bulletin board. *My Susan, she can fly*. And then you drew a
heart.

After Flying in a Yellow Plane to the San Diego Airport

you will stand on a curb
with a backpack and pup tent
and wait with people you know
by their calm and open faces
are going to the same place,
a monastery where a festival
of one-thousand people will coil
in long lines at bathrooms
and the dining hall and rattlesnakes
will crawl through the women's campground,
after you vow to be silent for five days,
and then the rains will come
as gentle finger taps, then cymbals
and drums, and the valleys and hills
will go gray to match the sky,
and when you wake at 6 a.m. to the sound
of a nun singing and ringing a deep gong,
you will rise to walk with a throng of meditators
led by a Vietnamese monk who you will never see,
but you will be swallowed by a stillness,
like diving underwater to swim the length
of a pool, a quiet so loud it throbs.

Haiku in Solitude

"Do introverts get
lonely?" Dogs don't answer, snore
on floor by queen bed.

"Make More Love" wall art
laughs above my pillowed head,
hung before breakup.

Hugless in Phoenix
cuddles chiweenie's silk fur,
inhales musk and warmth.

Masks dangle key rack:
floral, lip prints, checkered; three
are grandgirl's, three mine.

Gray birds perch upper
branches of yellow ash tree,
look down. I look up.

Dear Grief,

Get out and take what you brought:
my granddaughter's nightmares, her need
to hold my hand so she can sleep;

the old Lhasa Apso's congested heart,
its high-grade murmur, all her meds,
especially the one now causing her to leave
fluorescent pee rings in the hall.

Take my rose-colored rearview mirror
and the words of a former therapist,
"Well, I think he's the only man you ever really loved."

Take that man's email from my spam folder,
his message, "This song made me think of you,"
link to a Simon & Garfunkel tune: "Old Friends."

Nonverbal bullets ricochet in my head,
Damn you! in response. Take my spam folder
and my inability not to peek.

Open all the windows and let in some light:
heart drawn on a paper-plate by my granddaughter,
plate taped to a popsicle stick, her directions, "Hold this

up to show people who you love," flock of rock doves
on the front porch that whoosh into the sky
as the door opens.   Leave the key.

About the Author

Susan Vespoli lives in Phoenix, Arizona, where she relies on the power of writing to stay sane. She's taught Montessori preschoolers and ENG101 to community college students, owned a school, delivered newspapers, bicycled up a mountain, rehabbed a few extreme fixer-upper houses, and currently facilitates virtual writing circles on writers.com. Her work has been published in *Rattle, Mom Egg Review, Nasty Women Poets: An Unapologetic Anthology of Subversive Verse, Nailed Magazine,* and other cool spots.

Find her at https://susanvespoli.com/

www.ingramcontent.com/pod-product-compliance
Lightning Source LLC
Chambersburg PA
CBHW071357090426
42738CB00012B/3150